The Journey of Peace and Purpose

JEREMY WRIGHT

The Journey of Peace and Purpose

ISBN 978-1-66787-187-5 (Print)

ISBN 978-1-66787-188-2 (eBook)

Dedicated to:
Anyone who desires a life of peace and purpose.

This workbook includes improved work from previous books:
- *A Gift of Peace and Purpose: A Survivor's Journey*
- *Love and Meditation: The Keys to Manifestation*
- *Lenses: Seeing the Unseen Spaces Between Us*
- *Well to the Soul: Pouring from a Full Vessel*
- *Hidden Meadows: The Fulfilled Promise*
- *Compass of Love: The Journey of Peace and Purpose*

Workbook Intention

The intention of this workbook is to offer an easily applied approach to the journey of peace and purpose through self-reflection. As a hands-on learner, I understand that reading books can be challenging, especially when they are hundreds of pages long. With this self-paced workbook as the conclusion to the *Peace and Purpose* series in this form, my hope, in the end, is that you walk away with: a new perspective on life, knowledge of how to obtain inner peace, and the desire to chase your life's purpose. You can live the life you deserve by operating from a place of inner peace and making consistent and conscious choices to chase purpose. Before we get into doing the work, I provide further explanation for specific topics by laying a foundation for you to stand on; I encourage you to remain open-minded, as this may challenge your norms in a good way.

Brief highlights from books in the *Peace and Purpose* series are used to guide you on this journey. Across several books, I created constructs that I labeled as books of life, self, love, and meditation. To make these constructs easy to understand, they are broken into chapters with quotes, mantras, and analogies. This workbook, along with *Hidden Meadows: The Fulfilled Promise*, reorganized these books and chapters in order from birth to death to ensure an understandable timeline of life is depicted for you.

This workbook is not the absolute answer to life but a tool to help navigate this human experience. Taking the time to get through this workbook is a signal to life that you are asking for more, whether knowingly or unknowingly. Let what you ask for be a life of peace and purpose that will sustain you and the generations behind you. Let the work you do in this workbook be a part of your ongoing journey to be the best version of yourself. Live the life you deserve by consistently honoring your life's purpose, being of service to people, and making the world better than it was when you were born.

Dear Me,

We did it! The initial idea of writing a book about our personal journey of peace and purpose grew significantly. This book that grew into a series of books was written with positive intent to help make this human experience easier to understand. Our goal was to write so that readers would take away lessons learned from our journey, reflect on their life, and be more intentional about their choices. It's fair to say that this was not an easy journey, but one well worth it.

By choosing consistency over perfection, we are proof that you can overcome generational trauma and cycles and leave a lasting, positive impression that will affect future generations. I feel our transparency in being imperfect has allowed readers to see the importance of giving oneself the grace and space necessary to do inner work. Being an imperfect example of what's possible when making the consistent and conscious choice to obtain inner peace and chase purpose, will yield abundance in many forms. Not just materialistically but more importantly, limitless opportunities in life. The foundation this book series created will be strong enough to handle anything we pursue afterward that is in alignment with our purpose.

Let's explore the impossible, for we have proven in writing this book series that things remain impossible when we do not take the first step in making them possible; even when the first step is unclear. Let's push beyond our comfort zone and step into the place the creator designed for us. Let's remember to give ourself the grace and space necessary to continue our personal work as we honor our purpose in life. The Peace and Purpose series in the form of self-help books and this workbook may be finished for now, but the work will remain ongoing.

With all the unconditional love from within,
The ME behind me

Dear Reader,

This workbook is your safe space to be free and not judged. The journey you are about to dive into will be challenging, yet worth every step you take if you see it through to the end. You may have never been given an opportunity or allowed yourself to choose yourself for your entire life. This realization about your life is where your journey begins, with self. When you finish this workbook, you may not have all the answers, but you will have taken many steps to be your best self, eventually leading to a life of peace and purpose.

Again, this is not an easy or overnight process; please accept that. I will also share with you that this may cause necessary discomfort in areas of your life. This workbook intentionally goes to the places within us that we keep hidden, whether we realize it or not. You must go to these places to address trauma, projections, and conditioning to obtain inner peace. Trust yourself enough to do so, knowing that you have survived this far in your life.

Embrace who you are in this moment. Be grateful to this person and give yourself permission to get to the core of who you are, which may mean releasing who you thought you were and the things deeply tied to that person. Obtaining inner peace through intentional and consistent efforts to heal and release what has held you back allows the core of who you are to leverage your new perspective on life, encouraging you to chase purpose and live the life you deserve. I am in awe of your ability to make it this far in life. The work to live the life you deserve starts from within and shows up in your behaviors as you endure this human experience. There are limitless possibilities with inner peace and chasing the purpose of your life.

With all of the unconditional love that I have,
Jeremy

Author Updates

I feel very aligned and in flow with my life's purpose of helping people operate at their highest potential through self-awareness. This doesn't mean that everything, including myself, is perfect. It does mean that because I operate from a place of inner peace, I know what honoring my purpose should feel like. My consistent and conscious choices to chase purpose required a state of mind and state of being that matched my inner peace. This required that I take time to breathe and fill my capacity by doing things that matched what inner peace felt like to me.

This reset allowed me to keep trusting the process, release to receive, build the stamina to chase my purpose, and believe wholeheartedly that abundance was my portion given my positive intention. When I submitted to life or found my flow, unimaginable things began to happen in a way that only divine chaos could manifest. I received my first check as an author, which means so much to me, given that I put in years of hard work. Events in my home state of South Carolina helped me realize how places and people like the future International African American Museum, Denmark Vesey, and James Baldwin shape my life. I met Charlamagne the God, a radio personality turned strategic investor from South Carolina who, in my opinion, is an example of the journey of peace and purpose.

Additionally, I started a doctoral program that, if finished, will help me with long-term goals. Lastly, I made it into Human Resources, specifically talent management. While in Corporate America, what better job to have than something that directly prepares me to honor my purpose outside of Corporate America? This job doesn't stop me from chasing my purpose outside of Corporate America; it helps me maintain alignment with my purpose. I no longer feel that my job and purpose pull me in two different directions. This helps life to bring other circumstances and people to mold and shape me in preparation for the place the creator designed for me to honor my purpose.

With restored capacity and alignment in my state of mind, state of being, and everyday life, I am ready to leap headfirst into each opportunity that aligns with my purpose. As I chase my purpose and see signs and symbols encouraging me to keep going, I remind myself that it is not about how and when things happen. It is about consistently and consciously operating from a place of peace while chasing purpose. I will not try to be perfect but consistent. This next phase of my life, a transition to abundance, is something I feel more than capable of handling and prepared for because I chose peace and purpose.

The Journey of Peace and Purpose

Before you start this workbook, I want you to practice grounding exercises. Grounding exercises are about using your senses as anchors to the present moment to slow down or stop thoughts that are happening in your mind. It is difficult to do the type of work you will do in this workbook if you do not have the mental space to do it due to the internal noise you have not learned how to manage. For most of you, this may be the first time you are practicing this; remember, it is about consistency in your practice, not perfection. We will learn how to further apply grounding exercises to daily life further in the workbook, but because it's so essential to helping you be present, I must put it at the beginning. Practice grounding exercises every possible moment.

Grounding Exercise Practice

Routinely practice these steps with a few of your senses to pull yourself into the present moment.

You need the following:

- Hearing: Water, chimes, or any instrumental sounds that are not distracting

- Smell: A candle, incense, or something that gives off a scent that you enjoy

- Touch: A necklace, bracelet, or object that has a texture that you can identify

Do the following:

- Hearing: Play the sound of choice at a comfortable volume

- Smell: Safely place your scented object within smelling distance

- Touch: Grab your object and get comfortable in a safe space

- Focus heavily on your senses (hearing, smell, and touch) with your eyes closed while practicing slow and deep breathing

After doing this for a few minutes, your mind should be still. Welcome to the present moment.

Book of Life

Abstract

You are a vessel consistently being molded and shaped by life to honor a divine and specific purpose or purposes. Through your purpose, you are contributing to the collective human experience in a way that only you can, with your uniqueness. As a vessel that is a human being, you are limited in your capacity in ways such as mentally, physically, and emotionally. We must demonstrate consistent behaviors to choose ourselves first, through self-love and self-care, ensuring an overflow in our capacity to get through this human experience and, more importantly, honor our purpose. Through consistent reflection or meditation, we must go within ourselves to understand the more profound meaning of the circumstances we find ourselves in and the people we interact with during this human experience. What we find within circumstances and people are often lessons that mold and shape us for our purpose; without enough capacity, we simply see it as life.

Our purpose requires certain ingredients to ensure its effectiveness. This is why we may be born to particular families or circumstances that we may perceive as not ideal. Remember, meditation on circumstances and people allow for life lessons to come forth. In my opinion, life lessons come to undo certain things that have happened within our family lines or further refine us for our purpose. The decisions of those who came before us and our own are why we are not always aligned with our purpose, thus requiring us to heal traumas and break cycles through inner work. Consider the significant possibility that if you are learning about capacity or purpose for the first time, those who came before you have directly and indirectly molded and shaped you with a limited capacity and no awareness of their own purposes, thus poorly shaping the lens that you view life through.

Understanding this makes it easy to see why you may have to undo things that have happened within your family lines that came in the form of trauma, projection, and conditioning to reveal life lessons that prepare you for purpose. A possible advantage of being born to certain family lines or circumstances are the gifts and talents we inherit or develop, making it easier for our purpose to be received by the world. Even with someone who is well-rounded and has sorted out their past, purpose requires constant molding and shaping through more circumstances and people, bringing about additional life lessons. Capacity is essential, because it creates the space to see life lessons that are often hidden beneath the surface of our human experience as well as the stamina to keep honoring our purpose. It takes great effort to survive in some of our lives, let alone push toward something of more-significant impact. Your intentional decision to do the latter can positively change your life, the lives of those around you, and the lives of those who come behind you.

Chapter of the Bigger Picture

Quote—"We are more connected than we admit; harming you is like harming myself, disrupting life and its process." (*Love and Meditation: The Keys to Manifestation*, p. 56)

Mantra—I live my life knowing I will receive the outcomes of my behavior.

Analogy—Trees are so beautiful in all of the seasons that they go through. Trees are beautiful from when a seed falls on to the ground until a mature tree falls down. As a result of being in survival mode, we do not see that trees from all across the world do many things but, for our sake, provide air to breathe. A tree from Japan, a tree from Brazil, and a tree from the United States are different, but the same. If we wipe out trees, then we wipe out life. People in all stages of our lives can be beautiful. From conception to death, we can be beautiful. As a result of being in survival mode, we do not see that people from all across the world do many things but, for our sake, provide a means to live for each other. A person from Japan, a person from Brazil, and a person from the United States are different, but the same. If we wipe out people, then we wipe out life. Just as trees are connected through their roots and the ground to serve a bigger purpose for life, we are connected in spirit to serve a bigger purpose for the human experience.

Foundation

Given the journey you are about to embark on, I felt it was essential to lay a foundation that suggests everything in life is connected. Embracing this gives you the awareness to see that life is not about survival but about connection, as circumstances and people have deeper meaning. These are lessons that mold and shape you for your purpose. Self-awareness begins when you realize you are experiencing life as a human being, although connected to everything spiritually. In other words, life is a game that consists of a character in the game and the player of the game. Self-awareness helps you realize you are the player of the game, not a character in the

10

game, and should see the circumstances and people in the game as preparation for your purpose. Too often, we operate as the character in the game and not the player of the game due to being in survival mode or having limited capacity, making it easy to miss life's connectedness and the bigger picture. This may not make sense now, but that's okay; just remember that everything in life is connected, and you are constantly being readied for your purpose.

Chapter of Purpose

Quote—"My soul bears my purpose as a gift to the world I was born in." (*Well to the Soul: Pouring from a Full Vessel*, p. 16)

Mantra—Every day, I wake up to honor my purpose; to be of service to others is fulfilling.

Analogy—What is the purpose of a computer or cell phone? Every person who owns a computer or cell phone could use it for a unique purpose, such as communication, business operations, or social media. What is consistent is that there are necessary components for each, consisting of hardware, software, a power source, and a user. This is very similar to us in our human expression during this human experience that we are having.

The outer human expression of who we are, or the physical, represents the hardware. The inner spiritual expression of who we are, or the nonphysical, represents the software. Our outer expression, just like computers and cell phones, can take on different shapes, colors, accessories, and sizes. Just like computers and cell phones, our inner expression can have different interfaces or ways of showing up. They both need one another to make it possible for the computer or cell phone to fulfill a purpose.

When the hardware or the software is out of balance, the computer or cell phone's capacity is limited, regardless of how well some components are working. This is true for your outer and inner expressions of self as well. When hardware surpasses its software or vice versa, there must be an upgrade through deliberate choices to better the whole and not just individual parts. To take it a step further, the whole made from these two parts is nothing without a source: electricity. The power source of our human experience is God or the creator.

Just like electricity does not tell the computer or cell phone what to do, in my experience, this is also true for God in our lives. God is simply the fuel of life and whatever we decide to do in our life is up to us, as we have free will or the ability to make decisions. As the user, knowing you will go through circumstances with people because of your initial decision must remain at the forefront of your free will. Whether your decision is aligned with your purpose or not, circumstances and people always prepare you for your purpose while bringing what you have asked for, both knowingly and unknowingly. This highlights the importance of self-awareness, operating from our highest sense of self, to make more-favorable decisions in alignment with our purpose.

The difference between users within our human experience is our constrained experiences or capacities due to the ongoing battle between systems, nature, and humanity. This ongoing battle has conditioned us to think that our power source is the achievement or acquisition of things. As users, we must remain connected to the source to ensure harmonic rhythm by leading with our highest sense of self. Your highest sense of self must create a harmonic rhythm between your outer and inner expression while fueled by the power source of life: God. The decisions you make dictate the outcomes of the whole. If there is a balance between all parts, the whole can align its outcomes with a purpose that can change the world. In alignment with and by God, and with enough capacity, you operating as your highest sense of self can use your personality, way of thinking, way of learning, smile, hands, lessons learned, gifts, and talents, along with everything that makes you unique, to honor your purpose in a way that only you can.

Foundation

From *Lenses: Seeing the Unseen Spaces Between Us*, I mentioned a Japanese term, *Ikigai*, which suggests that your purpose is something you love, that the world needs, something you are good at, and something you can be paid for. I believe that our purpose sits at the intersection of our lessons learned, gifts and talents, and how we are of service to people. There is a thread that can be traced through these things if we have the capacity to reflect on how life is connected, as we are being molded and shaped through circumstances and people. You must see between the unseen spaces with the right perspective on life to move forward with what you need to honor your purpose; this is why capacity and self-awareness are so important.

The ability to realize you are not your physical body, thoughts, emotions, circumstances, or trauma is critical to this journey. These happen within the human experience, but are not who you are. You are the awareness that is experiencing life; the hidden quiet observer waiting to step forward to help bring peace, clarity, and direction to your human experience. For your entire life, you have been conditioned and taught to believe you are the character in the game, the computer, or the cell phone; let's shift your perspective to help give context to circumstances and people in your life, making it easy to identify and honor your purpose.

Chapter of Life as a Process

Quote—"No matter how or when you bring water to a boil, one must have and use everything necessary to make it happen; trust the process." (*Lenses: Seeing the Unseen Spaces Between Us,* p. 15)

Mantra—I trust the process and allow it to unfold without concern about the how and when.

Analogy—Have you seen a lion in person, without a cage? I imagine it is nothing to shrug at, as your life can change in seconds. Everyone is obsessed with the lion as the king of the jungle, but rarely stops to think about the process it takes to become king of the jungle. From a cub to an adult, the lion cannot take shortcuts; doing so can be the difference between life and death.

Foundation

Before we transition into doing the work required on the journey of peace and purpose, let's embrace consistency over perfection. This journey is not about being perfect but constantly realizing that even in what you perceive as good, bad, and ugly, you are being readied for your purpose through your circumstances and people. Trust the no, which could be a blessing and a redirection. Trust the delay in getting the desires of your heart, which could be additional preparation to handle what you want. Trust your highest sense of self as the best decision maker of your life, as it is connected to God or source. Everything happens for a reason; without the self-awareness to see it, circumstances and people in your life are just markers of moments of you trying to survive during this human experience. From a place of self-awareness, make the best decision with what you have and trust the process to unfold to your purpose.

I encourage you to embrace that you have multiple lenses that you can view life through; we will define this very shortly. Let's revisit the process of life as seen in *Lenses: Seeing the Unseen Spaces Between Us* by first giving my definition of components that make up our life experiences and how they work together. I encourage you to redefine the components of life to make sense for you and what you choose to believe.

- **Source**: To me, source is the collective of everything. It is you, it is me, it is the animals, it is the trees, it is grass, it is water, it is the clouds, it is the asteroid, it is the stars, it is. Source is not he, source is not she, source is not angry, source is not happy, source simply is. Suppose source could be anything, according to the laws that hold together our human experience. In that case, you must balance what you recognize source as. The presence of two halves makes a whole, and thus source is. Source is everything beyond what you define source as, meaning it is incomprehensible, so I simply say source is. We are responsible for labeling and defining things in a way that makes us feel comfortable to comprehend, determining if it is a threat to our lives. This doesn't mean letting everything fall apart but instead means taking a step back, breathing, and being okay with things not fitting within our ability to comprehend and fix. Rest comfortably in the fact that source will provide a never-ending flow of limitless possibilities whether we choose to honor our purpose or not; the choice is ours.

- **Highest Sense of Self**: To me, the highest sense of self is an internal spiritual expression of source. It is our never-ending connection to source, making us spiritually limitless. We, unlike source, are physically limited in this human experience. Given that we are source and possess a fraction of source, we can navigate life easily if and only if we make room for our highest sense of self to step forward and guide our actions. This limitless spiritual expression connects us all and gives us abilities beyond the comprehension of the human expression. We limit ourselves based on our ability to comprehend through the physical lens. We can shift to our spiritual lens to see limitless possibilities and the unseen spaces between us.

- **Purpose**: To me, purpose is your reason or reasons for being or your way to be of service to the collective human experience. To ensure it is obvious, I'll restate that purpose is not self-serving but an opportunity to serve others. It takes work to identify your purpose. This is especially true when you are not aware of any lens other than your physical lens to see. You will know when you have landed on your purpose based on the way it feels and what happens when you are of service to people with good intentions. As I stated in *Love and Meditation: The Keys to Manifestation*, "Chase your purpose and everything will follow. Chase everything and life will bring you sorrow." (p. 8)

- **Time and Chance**: To me, I would define time as a continuous spectrum of events that consist of circumstances and people. As things unfold, there is a precise moment when circumstances and people align just right, creating chance. I am growing to accept that time, as we have defined it in everyday life, is a false reality. We have defined time to help us be productive, but it doesn't have to be that way; we choose for it to be that way. Think of life beyond you. Think of the duck in a pond, the shooting star in the sky, and the trees as they go through seasons. These things do not adhere to what we have defined as time; they simply unfold without worrying about the how or when. I don't know about you, but it is infrequent that I see a duck, star, or tree in distress unless an outside force brings that stress on to it. Just as source simply is, everything outside of our life simply is, without adhering to what we define as time; they seem to be just fine. The difference between these things and us is our connection to source, our highest sense of self. Appropriately and intentionally using our higher sense of self makes life easier. Circumstances that involve people create chances, and thus opportunities necessary for us to be readied for our purpose. We often overlook these unseen spaces between us and end up in a cycle of unlearned lessons.

- **Circumstances and People**: To me, circumstances are a brief snapshot of our life with context. We choose to make circumstances good, bad, or ugly. Circumstance is none of these things; it simply is. People are literally all seven billion of us on this rock we call earth. As stated before, circumstances and people have underlying lessons tied to them that, hopefully, you learn early on in life rather than later. We cannot learn everything, and that is okay. We can simply do our best to identify, learn, and apply life lessons to be our best selves and be readied for our purpose.

- **Life Lesson**: To me, a life lesson is a piece of knowledge hidden within circumstances and people that is necessary to equip you to handle your purpose. Without this knowledge, you will not handle your purpose well. Purpose is exceptionally dense and impactful; you must equip yourself to handle it. It's almost like each life lesson you learn gives you a key ingredient to the recipe that illuminates your purpose. There are many life lessons, and I am inclined to say that we will always learn and grow on our spectrum of unfolding events. It wouldn't be life if these life lessons were right before us to quickly identify, learn, and apply. The hidden nature of life lessons makes it possible for cycles to be created.

- **Cycle**: To me, a cycle is an unlearned lesson, within a circumstance, potentially passed down from one generation to the next. It's very plain and straightforward: what my grandparents learned or did not learn is passed down to my parents through their actions. What my parents did or did not learn is passed to me through their actions. It is up to me to choose to do things differently, hopefully through self-awareness. When you shift from the physical to a spiritual lens, you can clearly see what needs to be done to break cycles. Once you become self-aware, it becomes a question of whether you have the capacity and then drive to break the cycle. Sometimes cycles are created through events that affect us deeply. The holistic experience of this impact is what I consider trauma.

- **Trauma**: To me, trauma is an event or series of events on your spectrum of unfolding events that are so impactful emotionally and physically that they create a void. Sometimes the trauma is so significant that our human expression cannot deal with it. Thus, we fracture our lens. We should continue to make addressing trauma, projects, and conditioning normal; going to therapy to help get to the root of our issues. Going the extra mile to find the right mental health professional for what we have experienced and committing to putting forth the genuine work to be our best selves can be life changing for generations. Our mental health is critical to our survival during this human experience. When we do not address trauma, the void on the unfolding spectrum of events begins to affect your life in ways that may not have been intended.

  Imagine walking on a trail, and you trip and get back up. Tripping on this trail represents trauma or a void being created. Getting back up without checking to ensure you did not hurt yourself represents suppressing what has happened to you, even if you do not intend to do so. The further you walk down that trail without addressing the trauma, the bigger the void, making the journey more difficult. Sometimes trauma can cause us to be mentally held captive in that void on our spectrum, but we physically have moved forward because life does not stop. This misalignment can create an impact beyond what we realize.

  Unfortunately, we are left with a choice because some of the things we have defined to measure productivity—such as time and profit margins—do not always consider human experience. Get up and keep walking or get left behind. When the choice is made to get up and keep walking, we eventually end up being swallowed by our void without realizing it. That void can appear in many forms, such as anxiety, stress, depression, and more. Eventually, we create a sense of false reality that we operate within, looking through a fractured lens; this becomes our norm unless we choose to address it.

I felt this when I experienced a family member dying by suicide for the first time; I was given three days for bereavement from my job without tapping into other resources such as Family Medical Leave or the grace of people with influence. Not knowing the importance of mental health, I returned to work in a daze, only to be negatively impacted by the stress of work and life itself. I didn't know that I was sinking into a void that was crippling my ability to get through life; I was just trying to survive.

- **Norms**: To me, norms are our consistent reality based on what we have experienced in our life. What I consider normal may be different from what you consider normal. My norm was a tiny nuclear family in which I was the only child for an extended time. My grandparents spoiled me, my aunt and I were like Bonnie and Clyde, and my mom was an unstoppable force that made something out of nothing. Of course, I had other family members and friends. Still, the number of people I spent most of my life with during my younger years was minimal. This sharply contrasts with someone who is used to two parents in the family, brothers and sisters, cousins, all four grandparents, aunts, uncles, and more. I would be in total shock and probably sit in a corner if I was put in this situation, because that is not my norm based on my life experiences. From this, we get a glimpse at the unseen spaces between me, who was raised with a small family, and someone who was raised with a bigger family. How I approach things because of what was normal to me may differ from how they approach things. Guess what? That is okay! Our norms begin to shape how we interact within circumstances and with people. This becomes the lens that we look out of, even when that lens is fractured.

- **Lens:** To me, your lens is how you view or process things and operate based on your norms. We should be mindful that it is possible to view things from varying places on your spectrum of events. Remember, there is a possibility of you being misaligned mentally and physically; you always view things based on your lens. In other words, wherever you are mentally on your spectrum of life events, combined with what is normal to you, is the lens through which you view your present circumstances. Your physical or survival lens is always there, as it is required for you to make it through life. We aren't always aware of our spiritual lens, which helps us see the more profound meaning of circumstances and people. Unless taught, until an event causes us to see through that lens or we are naturally programmed to see through that lens, we view everything through our physical or survival lens, making it easy to miss life lessons presented as circumstances and people. Again, it can be difficult to shift between lenses, especially when something traumatic has happened on your spectrum of unfolding events. When we have a fractured physical lens, often due to a traumatic event or current circumstances, we cannot do things that align us with an outcome outside of a cycle or intentionally toward our purpose. Our lens, physical or spiritual, helps us to make decisions in our life.

- **Decisions:** To me, a decision is walking down a particular path when presented with opportunities during an event on your spectrum of unfolding events; it is a choice. To be consistent, there is no good, bad, or ugly decision; it's simply a decision. Beyond

21

this decision are both effects we are aware of and some we are not. The impacts of our decision will always come back to us, as this is how life unfolds. The goal is to make decisions aligned with your purpose in life. This is not always easy; especially given the lens you look through maybe compromised or you are not aware of the right lens to look through.

- **Life Experience**: To me, life experience is the totality of what you experience during your life, up until the present moment. How far you look at the spectrum of unfolding events gives you context for why things are the way they are. An example of this is where you are right now in your life. Within the past thirty days, anything and everything that has happened helps you understand your life from a limited view. When you widen that view to maybe your entire life, it is possible to understand through your experience with life why you do what you do. We define the things we encounter in life as good, bad, and ugly. Still, I encourage you to not box in your life experiences, regardless of how narrowly or widely you may look at them. When we look at our life through a physical lens, we do not see the deeper meaning of circumstances and people. Remember that you are a small piece of source which simply is. It is necessary to strengthen your ability to shift to your spiritual lens to see the unseen spaces between us.

Formulas

- (Your Highest Sense of Self + Your Purpose) + Time and Chance (Circumstances and People + Decisions) = Your Birth

- Your Birth × (Family Trauma × Family Cycles) = Your Norms

- Your Norms + (Circumstances and People + Your Decisions) + (Your Trauma + Your Cycles) = Your Lens

- Your Birth × Your Norms × Your Lens (Circumstances and People + Your Decisions) = Life Experience

- Life Experience ÷ (Circumstances + People) = Your Life Lessons

- Your Life Lessons + Application + Gifts + Talents + Service to Others = Your Life Purpose

- Your Life Purpose + Collective Life Purpose of All Human Experiences = Source

Chapter of Forming My Lens

Quote—"I can see a lot and still not understand until its meaning is revealed." (*Lenses: Seeing the Unseen Spaces Between Us,* p. 24)

Mantra—I am forever evolving to become my best self; my perspective and understanding evolve with me.

Analogy—We were illiterate until we were taught what letters and numbers are and, more importantly, how to use them to derive meaning. Being taught, by self or others, is what forms your understanding to become literate. When the way you are taught is tainted, the way you derive meaning is also tainted. Unfortunately, you go through life at a disadvantage, not deriving true meaning from what you experience until you take action.

Do the Work

Given that we have free will, it is truly up to us to allow our highest sense of self to make the best choices for us in alignment with our purpose. Through self-awareness, our highest sense of self has the space to help us see the connectedness and deeper meaning of circumstances and people in our lives. The deeper meaning of circumstances and people, often lessons, molds and shapes us for our purpose. Remember, our lens is formed based on our norms; those who came before us help create our norms. Let's take a moment to reflect on lessons that I learned during my journey of peace and purpose after shifting my lens. I hope this encourages self-reflection about lessons you are being taught to ready you for your purpose.

Lessons from Self: Wake Up

Take a moment to reflect on possible lessons that you need to learn about yourself.

- Is there a set of circumstances or people in my life that causes me to reflect on the decisions that I have made?

- If multiple circumstances and people cause me to reflect on my decisions, what do they have in common?

- What underlying lesson, when applied, could prevent me from being in the same circumstances or dealing with the same people?

- What would happen if I missed the lesson?

- Why do I think these circumstances or specific people are necessary for me?

- As a part of this circumstance, what lesson could I be to this person's life?

- Now that I see the unseen space between the circumstance, the person(s), and me, what do I need to keep, stop, and start doing?

Lessons from Relationships: Be Intentional and Use Your Voice

Take a moment to reflect on possible lessons that you need to learn about relationships.

- Is there a person that causes me to be uncomfortable or challenges me? Why?

- Is there a person that I am drawn to positively, because I want them to grow or see something in them? Why?

- In either situation, what are the common characteristics of our interactions?

- What underlying lesson or message could be intended to be given or received?

- What would happen if this person or I missed the lesson?

- Why do I think these circumstances or specific person(s) are necessary?

- Now that I see the unseen space between the circumstance, the person(s), and me, what do I need to keep, stop, and start doing?

Lessons from Work: Be Optimistic

Take a moment to reflect on possible lessons that you need to learn about what you do for work.

- Considering that there are millions of jobs available, why am I currently working where I am?

- What opportunity does this job provide for circumstances and people to come into my life and help me toward my purpose?

- Am I in a position where I can help other people pursue their purpose?

- What could be the underlying reason I am at this job as a part of the circumstances in my life that may involve people?

- What would happen if I missed the reason?

- Why do I think these circumstances or specific person(s) are necessary?

- Now that I see the unseen space between the circumstance, the person(s), and me, what do I need to keep, stop, and start doing?

Lessons from Life: Love Yourself, Be Present, Be Patient, and Be Resilient

Take a moment to reflect on possible lessons that you need to learn from everyday living.

- Does my lens need attention?

- What are things I now realize?

- Why do I think these circumstances or specific person(s) are necessary based on what I have been through?

- What do these lessons, circumstances, and people have in common?

- How can I be of service to people with my lessons learned, gifts, and talents?

- What would happen if I did not serve people with my purpose in life?

- Now that I see the unseen space between myself, the circumstance, and the person(s), what do I need to keep, stop, and start doing?

As briefly mentioned earlier, we are always asking for things, both knowingly and unknowingly. For each of the lessons above disguised as circumstances, reflect on these questions:

- What am I asking for intentionally and unintentionally through my thoughts, words, and actions?

- What is my current circumstance(s) that bring discomfort?

- Who are the people in my life?

- What was the outcome of me applying my lessons learned?

Self-Reflection

To ensure you understand the book of life and recognize what is at stake if you do not pursue inner peace and the purpose of your life, reflect on the following:

- How do I play a part in the reason I believe people exist?

- After finding the connection between the ingredients of purpose (learned life lessons, gifts, and talents), how can I be of service to people?

- What can I start, stop, and keep doing, knowing that life is a process I must trust?

- How might my perspective and understanding need to evolve, given that I accept that life is a process and that circumstances and people condition me to be ready for my purpose?

Application

After reflecting on your answers to the above questions, journal about these responses for at least fifteen minutes per day. If you need more time to reflect and journal, do so; this is your opportunity to check your understanding of life and what's at stake when a journey of peace and purpose is not taken.

Grounding Exercise Practice

Routinely practice these steps with a few of your senses to pull yourself into the present moment.

You need the following:

- Hearing: Water, chimes, or any instrumental sounds that are not distracting

- Smell: A candle, incense, or something that gives off a scent that you enjoy

- Touch: A necklace, bracelet, or object that has a texture that you can identify

Do the following:

- Hearing: Play the sound of choice at a comfortable volume

- Smell: Safely place your scented object within smelling distance

- Touch: Grab your object and get comfortable in a safe space

- Focus heavily on your senses (hearing, smell, and touch) with your eyes closed while practicing slow and deep breathing

After doing this for a few minutes, your mind should be still. Welcome to the present moment.

Book of Self

Abstract

Earlier, I mentioned an ongoing battle of systems versus humanity versus nature; as of now, the systems are winning. Systems are winning because they have conditioned each generation behaviorally to survive by any means necessary through chasing achievement, possessions, and a comparatively brief moment of a peaceful retirement. This may explain why you may never have heard of capacity or purpose: those who raised you did the best they could with what they had. Our conditioning has engrained comparison into our behavior, as who we are may be less than what society is willing to accept due to a false status quo. This makes it easier to look at others to project and feel better on the surface, but with the hidden intent of distracting us from our shortcomings. Before we know it our lives have ended, and most people will have nothing to show for it beyond things that will eventually perish.

This is why we must consistently and consciously choose inner peace and chase our purpose in life over anything else. Our purpose is something that spans time, space, and energy if we honor it with good intentions during this human experience. Purpose can only be honored through a vessel that operates in authenticity, one that accepts who they are as an imperfect human being that is divine perfection. Embracing our imperfections, the bigger picture, and the process of life helps to disarm us, to stop projecting and comparing ourselves to others—as they too must honor their reason for being, in which we may play a part. Being our authentic selves and embracing our imperfections helps to create inner peace; sometimes it takes help from a mental health professional to get there, and that's okay. Knowing that life is about honoring our purpose, it is more advantageous to focus on being our best selves, to show up as individuals who have worked on themselves with the capacity to honor their purpose.

Boundaries are a cornerstone to showing up authentically and having the capacity to chase purpose. When systems have conditioned us to focus on achieving the status quo before honoring nature and humanity, it will feel unusual to establish boundaries. Recognizing when you need to restore your capacity starts with self-awareness, with remembering that we as human beings are limited in every way except spiritually. Capacity is also essential during the journey of peace and purpose because stamina will help you withstand how and when things will manifest. This consistent and conscious choice to chase purpose is only as strong as the foundation it stands on: you.

Chapter of Acceptance

Quote—"I did not have a choice to be born. I do have a choice in how I show up every day. I choose to be secure in who I am; there is no other way." (*Well to the Soul: Pouring from a Full Vessel,* p. 30)

Mantra—I am in love with the core of who I am and how I show up daily.

Analogy—One of the beauties of nature is how seasons change. There are indirect influences in how seasons shift, for example based on our habits, but for the most part seasons transition effortlessly. Seasons do not choose to change; it's an ongoing cycle of what we have grown to know as a part of life. We do not have a say in how seasons show up, but, regardless, this process will remain until it occurs differently, and we must embrace this.

Do the Work

Take a moment to reflect on the Chapter of Acceptance by answering the below questions.

- What are at least ten things that I love about myself?

- How would my life be different if these ten things were taken away?

- What are at least five things, different than above, that people love about me?

- How would my life be different if these five things were taken away?

- What would I change about myself, and why?

- If I could change anything about myself, what is the root of why I would change it?

- What would life look like if all the things I like about myself and all of the things that people like about me disappeared from all people?

- Suppose the things I would change about myself ended up being the same things everyone would change about themselves. Would I want to be different?

- Have external influences such as media, friends, or family shaped how I view myself?

- What outlets are present that help me embrace who I am? Do I seek and support them?

Chapter of the Human Spectrum

Quote—"Our uniqueness and imperfection qualify us as human; anyone who challenges another opens their soul like a window." (*Well to the Soul: Pouring from a Full Vessel*, p. 26)

Mantra—How I see other people reflects where I am in my personal journey.

Analogy—The sky is a beautiful thing. Day or night, you can see something new every time. What remains the same is that what you see will never be the same, yet we know it is the sky. There are different planets, moons, and stars that we may be able to see with our naked eye, but when we use the right tools, we can see even more. Beyond what we know as the sky, the known universe is an infinite possibility.

It is not possible to comprehend the known universe, but what is possible is that no two things are the same. I believe that God or source, in its infinite capability, created everything in a way that is not comprehensible, including human beings. Like the universe, we, as human beings, are infinite in possibility. The spectrum of who we are should be embraced just like the universe. No planet, moon, or star is better than the other, but acts as a part of a larger whole of infinite possibility. Is it possible to see each other as equals one day?

Do the Work

Take a moment to reflect on the Chapter of the Human Spectrum by answering the below questions.

- What is a human being to me?

- What is something that makes me uncomfortable about someone who may be of a different gender, race, or age, or have a background different from mine?

- What started this unease?

- Do I feel this represents everyone who may be associated with this facet of who they are?

- Is there something that I have in common with this group of people?

- Did I learn anything about this group of people from previous generations?

- Suppose I learned my point of view about these people from previous generations. What is the full context of why the previous generation developed their opinions?

- What would my life look like if all of this group's contributions were taken away?

- If I was a part of this group, how would I want people to treat me, considering I may not have a choice in why someone may not like certain things about me?

- How do I want future generations of this group to treat me and my future generations?

Chapter of Boundaries

Quote—"A boundary is a request for protection from one person to another." (*Well to the Soul: Pouring from a Full Vessel*, p. 34)

Mantra—I have healthy boundaries to maintain my inner peace and capacity to chase purpose.

Analogy—Elements such as air, earth, fire, and water have existed for longer than we have. We have grown to embrace them as a part of our lives, using them to survive. What is unsaid about the relationship between elements and us is a boundary of respect. At any moment, the elements, or we as humans, could create an imbalance within the other causing harm. Respecting this boundary between the elements and ourselves should be present among us as humans; we need each other to stay alive.

Do the Work

Take a moment to reflect on the Chapter of Boundaries by answering the below questions.

- What does a boundary mean to me?

- Based on my life, why is it important that I establish boundaries?

- What does it mean when a boundary I have set is not respected?

- How does it feel when my boundaries are violated?

- What would people think if I established a healthy boundary, explaining that it was for my benefit, part of my process to living a better life?

- Have I seen people in my life establish healthy boundaries?

- Who in my life is good at setting and enforcing healthy boundaries?

- Is there a difference in the quality of their life compared to mine, given that healthy boundaries are established and enforced?

- Have I knowingly violated someone else's boundary?

- What is more important to me, enforcing my boundaries or taking care of other's needs before mine?

Chapter of Pouring

Quote—"What I am pouring into will carry the intention and condition in which I pour. I pour when my intention and condition are right so that what I pour into can grow." (*A Gift of Peace and Purpose: A Survivor's Journey*, p. 42)

Mantra—I am pouring my purpose as a gift to the world, watering seeds that will bloom.

Analogy—What we drink and eat directly affects our human expression. Our physical and mental well being reflect the purity of the things we consume. This parallels with pouring our gifts into people and people pouring into us, capacity full or not. Even when we have the capacity to pour with pure intention, people may not have the capacity to receive; the opposite is true as well. If we are expecting something from someone, we should consider their capacity, as they may not be able to give what we expect. When a vessel is contaminated, impaired, or does not have the capacity, we should consider the impact of our actions and expectations. Do not run the risk of contaminating the well being of ourselves and those who we pour into.

Do the Work

Take a moment to reflect on the Chapter of Pouring by answering the below questions.

- Am I ready to go on a journey of chasing my purpose without concern about how and when it may tangibly manifest?

- Am I willing to give myself continuous grace on the journey of chasing purpose?

- Is there something I am unwilling to sacrifice on this journey of chasing purpose?

- Is my life, as it is, something I—and future generations—would be proud of?

- What would it mean if I could identify my soul's purpose and live the life I feel I deserve due to pouring it into the world?

Self-Reflection

To ensure you understand the book of self and recognize what is at stake if you do not pursue inner peace and the purpose of your life, reflect on the following:

- Given that I must heal myself and evolve in some areas, what must I accept about my life and myself, knowing that my uniqueness qualifies me to honor my purpose?

- Knowing that the collective human experience is God or source, and the only way I can be prepared for my purpose is through circumstances that bring lessons, what must I start, stop, and keep doing when interacting with people?

- What boundaries must I set to restore, strengthen, increase, and protect my capacity to honor my purpose and live life as I please?

- What is my indication that I am in a balanced place to pour my purpose, being of service to people and making the world better?

Application

After reflecting on your answers to the above questions, journal about these responses for at least fifteen minutes per day. If you need more time to reflect and journal, do so; this is your opportunity to check your understanding of self and what's at stake when a journey of peace and purpose is not taken.

Grounding Exercise Practice

Routinely practice these steps with a few of your senses to pull yourself into the present moment.

You need the following:

- Hearing: Water, chimes, or any instrumental sounds that are not distracting

- Smell: A candle, incense, or something that gives off a scent that you enjoy

- Touch: A necklace, bracelet, or object that has a texture that you can identify

Do the following:

- Hearing: Play the sound of choice at a comfortable volume

- Smell: Safely place your scented object within smelling distance

- Touch: Grab your object and get comfortable in a safe space

- Focus heavily on your senses (hearing, smell, and touch) with your eyes closed while practicing slow and deep breathing

After doing this for a few minutes, your mind should be still. Welcome to the present moment.

Book of Love

Abstract

The human experience that we are a part of requires a connection. I feel that one of the things that connect us as human beings is love in its many forms. To me, love is consistent, positive action rooted in a good intention to be of service to self and then others. Learning that love is an action helps you recognize the level of effort required of yourself and others to love others and yourself. Love is not just words that make you feel good in the moment.

How you define love should be what you measure your relationships with, including the relationship with yourself. Just remember that people have a choice not to return love to you if it doesn't match or is not compatible with their own definition of love. When we do not recognize that love is an action, communication serves as the next best thing. In other words, when someone says, "I love you," this serves as love and is not the action of love. This lip service, saying things with no action, leads to broken hearts, trauma, and other negative emotions and experiences.

Our ability to be whole and authentic human beings is hinged on our needs. When specific needs are not being met, it may hinder our ability to show up in a way favorable to ourselves and others, making interactions challenging. This may give context to the way people show love and communicate, as well as their interactions within this human experience. When people's needs are met, it becomes easier to be whole and thus be love in action. Love, communication, and needs are connected because we as human beings need one another through interactions to learn the lessons that ready us for our purpose. Although honoring our life's purpose should be the primary goal, we should not forget to experience life as human beings. Live a life you will not regret. Experience love in all of its forms; you have free will.

Chapter of Love

Quote—"I love myself enough to show you that how I define love is essential to our relationship." (*Love and Meditation: The Keys to Manifestation*, p.18)

Mantra—I allow myself to experience the full spectrum of love.

Analogy—Weather is unpredictable. Things must be suitable for it to snow, and when they are not, snow will not happen. When we observe coldness in the air combined with enough moisture, we eventually experience snow falling. The action of Mother Nature makes it possible for us to experience snow. Regardless of what someone says, we must wait for the action of Mother Nature to make snowfall. It is the same for love; someone can say something that equates to love, but until we observe the individual's actions, we cannot experience love.

Do the Work

Take a moment to reflect on the Chapter of Love by answering the below questions.

- What have I observed, in terms of love, from those I was raised by?

- How do I define love?

- What are specific and recent examples of showing love to myself based on my definition?

- How often do I demonstrate my definition of love to myself?

- What will I commit to doing consistently to demonstrate love to myself?

- Write down at least five people who love me, based on how I define love, with a specific and recent example.

- How often do they demonstrate my definition of love to me?

- What are actions and words that, when used, make me feel someone does not love me?

- How do I show love to other people?

- How and when do I tell people how to love me or that I do not feel love from them?

- If I am in a romantic relationship, is it meeting my definition of love, and what will I do to change it if not?

- If I am not in a romantic relationship, am I ready for one? How must I prepare?

- Am I honoring peoples' definition of love as I expect them to honor my own?

- What do I need to start, stop, and keep doing in terms of love in all of its forms?

Chapter of Communication

Quote—"I choose to shape the sound from my lips to wrap around the shape of your heart." (*Love and Meditation: The Keys to Manifestation*, p.12)

Mantra—I am communicating for understanding and not to be heard.

Analogy—The intent of your message is a ship on its way to a destination. This destination is who you are trying to communicate with. Your ship must navigate the ocean, which is your message delivery. The unexpected icebergs, hurricanes, and remote islands in this ocean represent the perception and walls put up by the person or people you are trying to communicate with. Learn the path to your destination and plan for unexpected circumstances before you put up your sails on the way to your destination.

Do the Work

Take a moment to reflect on the Chapter of Communication by answering the below questions.

- What do I really want to say or, in other words, the true intent of my message?

- Have I looked at the situation objectively, with no emotions?

- Do I have specific examples of what I am trying to talk about?

- Have I considered the perspective of and impact on all parties involved?

- How does the receiver of my message prefer to communicate?

- How will the receiver of my message respond to my message?

- Is now the right time to have this conversation?

- Is the current setting the right setting to have the conversation?

- What do I want as an outcome of the conversation?

- Did I commit to the other person to help with the solution?

- How did the receiver of my message respond so that I know they received the intent of my message and understand my expectations?

Chapter of Needs

Quote—"People's needs are the framework for operating at their best self." (*Love and Meditation: The Keys to Manifestation*, p.17)

Mantra—I am fulfilling my core needs to be my best self.

Analogy—Have you ever seen a car run without gas or electricity? For a car to move, certain things must be readily available to work at their best. Without the proper maintenance, a brand-new car can be worthless and discarded, as it brings no value to those who need it. People are the same way; they have specific needs that must be in place to operate at their best self. Just as we take a car to a mechanic to understand what it needs to operate, we sometimes have to watch our own and other people's behaviors or simply ask them what they need. It is up to them, not you, to be a good steward of what is given to them to be their best self.

Do the Work

Take a moment to reflect on the Chapter of Needs by answering the below questions.

- Who taught me about or demonstrated healthy self-love and care to me?

- What is my indication that I need to take time for self-love and care?

- How can I communicate that I need to honor my needs?

- Am I prepared to be temporarily unavailable to others to honor my needs?

- How do I determine if I was clear in communicating my needs?

- Have I established a routine to ensure that I am honoring my needs?

- Am I honoring others' needs the way I expect them to honor my own?

Self-Reflection

To ensure you understand the book of love and recognize what is at stake if you do not pursue inner peace and the purpose of your life, reflect on the following:

- Have I consistently used my definition of love to hold myself and others accountable?

- What must I start, stop, and keep doing to ensure that my communication is clear?

- What is my indication that the needs of others or myself are not being met, preventing progress from being made?

Grounding Exercise Practice

Routinely practice these steps with a few of your senses to pull yourself into the present moment.

You need the following:

- Hearing: Water, chimes, or any instrumental sounds that are not distracting

- Smell: A candle, incense, or something that gives off a scent that you enjoy

- Touch: A necklace, bracelet, or object that has a texture that you can identify

Do the following:

- Hearing: Play the sound of choice at a comfortable volume

- Smell: Safely place your scented object within smelling distance

- Touch: Grab your object and get comfortable in a safe space

- Focus heavily on your senses (hearing, smell, and touch) with your eyes closed while practicing slow and deep breathing

After doing this for a few minutes, your mind should be still. Welcome to the present moment.

Book of Meditation

Abstract

This human experience we have as both human and spiritual beings is a lot. As it has become human nature to conquer, it seems an ongoing quest to conquer this human experience as it surpasses the comprehension of our humaneness. How does one navigate through life to consistently and consciously chase purpose? I believe the answer is inner peace. When we first started, and throughout this workbook, we practiced grounding exercises to help ground us into the present moment. The inner peace we experience in the present moment cuts through internal noise to create a bridge that connects our spiritual and human expression.

Once this bridge is established, we can leverage meditation to make space for our highest sense of self to step forward to help us navigate life through better decision-making. Through meditation, you can: ensure you make decisions in alignment with your purpose, connect with your loved ones who have passed on, dig to the root of issues within your life, receive direction and answers from the creator, and so many other things. Continue to embrace that you are a spiritual being having a human experience; you are connected to a divine and infinite source, God. This connection with God allows you to cocreate or manifest your life through the decisions you make with your human expression, hopefully guided by your highest sense of self.

Meditation also makes it easy to visualize with great detail, a key ingredient to manifesting. It provides the freedom to experience emotions you associate with what you visualize. Meditation gives you the space to see if your thoughts, words, actions, and emotions are in total alignment with what you are trying to manifest. I must emphasize without action on your part, you cannot manifest. You gain the most control over how you cocreate or manifest and navigate this human experience when your highest sense of self is making decisions based on precise alignment between the creator or source of this human experience, your internal spiritual expression, and your external human expression. Hopefully, by now, you know to choose your purpose by intentionally manifesting the circumstances and people that will mold and shape you to honor your purpose so that you can live the life you deserve.

To use an analogy, think of the unpredictable ocean, a ship, a first mate, and the captain. Life is the unpredictable ocean that has swells which in our everyday life represents circumstances and people that brings lessons and helps hone our gifts and talents. Your human expression is the ship that endures the swells of life and needs constant maintenance. Your spiritual expression in tandem with source or God is the first mate, who gives you direction and sometimes steps in through grace and mercy to keep the ship going. Your highest sense of self is the captain, who must always communicate with the first mate. When the captain submits to the ocean to learn lessons from its unpredictable nature and hones gifts and talents to navigate it, maintains the ship, and constantly communicates with the first mate, the captain is unstoppable.

If we do not meditate, we operate in survival mode, meaning we think we are the ship and try to stay afloat through the overwhelming swells of life without control or clear direction from the first mate or captain. Through meditation, we act as the captain who gets help from the first mate yet ultimately decides how to navigate the unpredictable ocean. The captain must: be present-minded at all times, go inward to get guidance and use instincts to make the best decisions, see and feel themselves arriving at the destination before they set off, check to make sure the ship is heading in the right direction, and keep going regardless of how little progress seems to be made eventually reaching the destination. As many say, you are the captain of your life; where will you go?

Chapter of Grounding

Quote—"Time is an illusion that has conditioned us to be productive. How can we be productive when our thoughts are in the past or future, and our bodies are present?" (*Love and Meditation: The Keys to Manifestation*, p.61)

Mantra—I am always at peace, and it feels still.

Analogy—When we buy food from the grocery store, there is always an expiration date. We can create many plans for this food, but it no longer serves its purpose to us once it is past its expiration date. What is ironic is that whether we choose to eat the food when we get it or right before it expires, what truly matters is when we decide to eat it. The moment we consume it, we experience its taste, texture, nutrients, and more. Grounding exercises are a way of pulling yourself to the present moment. Just as we cannot change when we purchase food, nor can we change when it expires, we must focus on the present moment.

Grounding Exercise Practice

Routinely practice these steps with a few of your senses to pull yourself into the present moment.

You need the following:

- Hearing: Water, chimes, or any instrumental sounds that are not distracting

- Smell: A candle, incense, or something that gives off a scent that you enjoy

- Touch: A necklace, bracelet, or object that has a texture that you can identify

Do the following:

- Hearing: Play the sound of choice at a comfortable volume

- Smell: Safely place your scented object within smelling distance

- Touch: Grab your object and get comfortable in a safe space

- Focus heavily on your senses (hearing, smell, and touch) with your eyes closed while practicing slow and deep breathing

After doing this for a few minutes, your mind should be still. Welcome to the present moment.

Chapter of Meditation

Quote—"If I could stop the world from moving, I am sure people wouldn't notice. The movement of the world doesn't make people move; people make themselves move." (*Love and Meditation: The Keys to Manifestation*, p.69)

Mantra—I am meditating in a place beyond space and time where things are clear.

Analogy—Throwing a rock into the water and trying to catch a ripple is like trying to catch a thought in your head. We cannot stop the ripple, but we can scoop some of the water into our hands. When we focus on what we have scooped out, we realize its stillness; it becomes our only focus, not the ripples beyond our control. Meditation is like the stillness of the water in our hands. It provides the space to think clearly and make sound decisions. It allows us to focus on small things to realize the connection to the collective. It allows us to dig deeply; this cannot be done in survival mode. Trying to get the ripples in a disturbance of water to calm is impossible, as the water decides when it will be still. This is often a true reflection of our life as we try to catch our thoughts, when we should simply be still and scoop out what we can control. From a place of optimism, clarity, and peace, focus on what you can control; make decisions that help you move forward in life.

Do the Work

Meditation comes in many forms. The important thing is finding a form of meditation that works for you. As stated in previous sections, it is about consistency, not perfection. Consider that you are an individual with many responsibilities in a hectic world. You are not an individual with the minimal, although essential, responsibilities of someone who lives a more secluded life, like a monk or a nun.

You may have many distractions that prevent you from what you may consider a perfect practice of meditation. I encourage you to research the best meditation form for you, and to practice it. I also recommend finding yoga studios, wellness events, and other opportunities to meet individuals who are trying to live a life that requires a practice that provides better quality of life. For me, meditation can be about deep and complex thoughts, supplementing the work being done with a mental health professional, or simply inner peace. Do what works for you with the intent of finding peace and purpose.

Chapter of Visualization

Quote—"What can be seen with my eye is not what I desire because it is already here. What I desire is a step beyond what my mind can fathom; it feels good to know that what is possible is within reach, as I already see it with my spiritual eyes." (*Love and Meditation: The Keys to Manifestation*, p.76)

Mantra—I clearly see the life of peace and purpose I desire to live.

Analogy—When we drive, we do not know our destination's condition until we get there. Regardless of what our navigation tells us, until we get there and see it with our naked eye, it is all hypothetical. The same faith we have for our destination to be there because we have been there a few times is the same faith we must have when seeing the impossible before it materializes. What you choose to do with your faith is up to you.

Do the Work

Be the kid who draws outside of the lines. Find ways to spark your creative genius. Put yourself in environments that allow you to be the wildly imaginative kid you were. Allow yourself the space to do what you were designed to do: create. The more you do this, the easier it becomes to visualize precisely what you want in your quest for peace and purpose.

Remember, what we ask for knowingly and unknowingly doesn't come back as blatantly as what we ask for, but as circumstances and people that come with hidden lessons. The more you spend time in meditation, co-creating the life you desire, the easier it becomes to see that it has always been a possibility; you just needed the space and capacity for it. Visualize in detail, like the paintings of Jean-Michel Basquiat, the writings of James Baldwin, the characters of Robin Williams, and the lyrics and singing of India.Arie. Allow yourself the freedom to see that everything is possible, and associate a general feeling that equates to it already being done. Feeling as if it's already done helps you with letting it go; do not obsess over it because that suggests lack or the opposite of it already being done. Things may not unfold exactly how you visualize them, but it will be more than enough for peace and purpose to be true.

Chapter of Posture

Quote—"Sitting incorrectly can limit oxygen intake; our posture must be correct to maximize what we are capable of." (*Love and Meditation: The Keys to Manifestation*, p.79)

Mantra—I give myself permission to experience emotions, mindful of my reaction.

Analogy—The best musicians, dancers, and athletes train tirelessly to perfect their craft. What we see when they perform results from countless hours of perfecting their gift or talent. Not breathing in enough air can cause a note to be impossible, not correctly timing a move can lead to being out of sync, and not stretching correctly can lead to a pulled muscle. Just as these individuals must practice a particular physical and mental posture to perfect their performance, we must also perfect a particular posture in every moment of our life. The result of what we see in moments of our life is because of the countless hours of the posture we have practiced.

Do the Work

I hope that it is clear that the journey of peace and purpose will not be easy. There will be moments when you question if it is worth the things you may endure. Awareness of how life sees you is critical, because it will be used as information that will reflect in the circumstances and people you encounter. This is why we focused heavily on self-awareness, grounding yourself in the present moment so you can identify when you need to take action or simply be still. It is not easy to be optimistic and blessed every day; the best advice I can offer is a familiar cliché: Gratefulness begets gratefulness.

Take a moment to reflect on the Chapter of Posture by answering the below questions.

- What are the emotions I feel when I am triggered?

- What can I do to pull myself to the present when I recognize that I am triggered?

- How can I communicate my needs to others in a moment of being triggered?

- Do I commit to positively reframing things that may be disheartening to the best of my ability?

- Do I commit to consistency over perfection?

Chapter of Manifestation

Quote—"If I think to breathe at my own pace before I change my pace of breath, which ultimately changes my breathing, I can obtain what I genuinely desire before working toward it." (*Love and Meditation: The Keys to Manifestation*, p.89)

Mantra—I live an abundant life of peace and purpose, which feels fulfilling.

Analogy—Changing a flat tire can be annoying, as it often delays what you are trying to accomplish. It can be challenging to jack up your car, remove your tire, replace it, and take the jack down. What's so ironic about this is that manifestation is the same way. We typically know what we must do before we start doing it. Still, nothing will happen until we start working toward it, even if we make mistakes and learn from them. We often have the right circumstances for what we want to manifest. We are really stopping the process from unfolding; not doing our part will never yield what we truly desire.

Do the Work

I use alignment and flow as ways to indicate if I am manifesting. To me, alignment is about creating a direct line between the creator and source of this human experience, your spiritual expression, your human expression, and your consistent behaviors. It suggests that you consistently and consciously choose peace and purpose over anything else. When you wake up in the morning, at work, in social settings, your thoughts, and in every area of your life, you are doing your best to be aligned with what you want to manifest; hopefully, that is peace and purpose. Again, this does not mean perfection; it means consistency.

This is where flow helps us to stay in touch with our emotions. To me, flow is leveraging the internal compass that we all have. It recognizes that when time and chance align to create opportunity, we check for alignment with what we want to manifest. The gut feeling of *This is or is not right for me*. Circling back to visualization, feeling as if it's already done, helps you to know when you are in flow and let it go after you have made your decision. Manifesting requires consistent work to meet life where it is trying to take you.

One of the ways that I try to create alignment and flow is by outlining my day in a way that makes the day easier. Knowing that we are all busy people, having a routine that involves checking and restoring your capacity, checking your posture, and creating alignment and flow makes manifesting peace and purpose easier. Below is an updated excerpt from *Love and Meditation: The Keys to Manifestation* of me, outlining my day. I encourage you to read and adapt it to your life. Even if you cannot dedicate as much time, remember that small amounts of time add up over time; find ways to divert time from social media, technology, or simple procrastination to live a life of peace and purpose.

My Routine

- Wake up with a soft alarm of a song that creates alignment and flow. By doing this, you signal to life that this is the energy, emotion, or vibration you want to match in circumstances and people. Do not wake up with an alarm clock blaring, rushed and in a panic; also, don't be late because of missing your alarm or hitting snooze.

    a. Examples include "Sacred Space" by India.Arie, "Be Alive" by Beyoncé, "Running (To You)" by Chike & Simi, and "I Am Everything" by Beautiful Chorus.

- While in bed, I ground myself into the present moment by acknowledging my physical body and the function of every part. I breathe in deeply and feel the sensation everywhere possible. By doing this, I have sent out gratitude for the function of my entire body.

- I acknowledge what I am grateful for: the ability to wake up in a safe environment, in my own bed, in my own apartment that I can pay for, all of my bills are paid in full, I lack for nothing, I have a career that is providing a means for me to get where I want to be and other things, my mom is alive and healthy, I will have a patient life partner who protects and provides, is emotionally available, communicates well, and loves me in the way that I need to be loved. By doing this I have just sent out gratitude for many things to the universe ("Give Thanks" by India.Arie and "Grateful" by Chris-n-Teeb).

- I start my hygiene practice and dedicate specific daily moments to my self-care.

- I go to my meditation area and ground myself further, state my affirmations, feel it as if it's already happening, visualize it, let it go, and commit to doing my part to make it come true. By doing this I have just released the energy of my affirmations becoming true ("Better Days" by Le'Andria Johnson" and "Bigger" and "Break My Soul" by Beyoncé).

- I start my day knowing that I have developed a routine to breathe and be present, to say my affirmations at 11:11 a.m., 1:11 p.m., immediately after work, and at 11:11 p.m.

- As I go throughout my day, things happen. But due to my morning routine, I have placed myself in a very clear space and know to look for circumstances and people to condition me for what I have asked for. I respond very intentionally by grounding myself in the present moment and allowing my highest sense of self to make the decision. By doing this, I have just sent out the most appropriate dispersal of energy during each situation at work. I remain as calm as possible when dealing with people. I maintain a posture of optimism ("Expect Your Miracle" by The Clark Sisters and "Energy" by Tyla Jane).

- Once I get finished with work, I wash the day off through grounding exercises and meditation and duplicate my morning routine of going to my meditation area to ground myself further, state my affirmations, feel it as if it's already happening, visualize it, let it go, and commit to doing my part to make it real. By doing this, I have just released the energy of my affirmations becoming true ("Three Little Birds" by Bob Marley).

- I take care of my body through working out (*Renaissance Act I* album by Beyoncé).

- I dedicate time to school, family, friends, and other things.

- I dedicate time to myself for whatever I want ("I Am" by Beautiful Chorus featuring India Arie).

- I dedicate time to moments of dancing and singing that I will share with my life partner.

  b. For example, I use songs like "Oh Me Oh My" by Aretha Franklin, "Here and Now" by Luther Vandross, "All the Man That I Need" by Whitney Houston, "The Right Kinda Lover" by Patti LaBelle, "Rock With You" by Michael Jackson, "Never Gonna Let You Go" by Faith Evans, "I Love Me Some Him" by Toni Braxton, "Raise the Bar" by Tamar Braxton, "That's When I Knew" by Alicia Keys, "Teachme" by Music Soulchild, "Spend My Life With You" by Eric Benét featuring Tamia, "Rather Be" by Brandy, "Plastic Off the Sofa" by Beyoncé, "No Letting Go" by Wayne Wonder …

- At the end of my night, I go to my meditation area to ground myself further, state my affirmations, feel if it's already happening, visualize it, let it go, and commit to doing my part to make it come true. By doing this, I have just released the energy of my affirmations becoming true.

- While in bed, I ground myself into the present moment by acknowledging my physical body and the function of every part. I breathe in deeply and feel the sensation everywhere possible. By doing this, I have sent out gratitude for the function of my entire body.

- I acknowledge what I am grateful for: the ability to wake up in a safe environment, in my own bed, in my own apartment that I can pay for, all of my bills are paid in full, I lack for nothing, I have a career that is providing means for me to get where I want to be and other things, my mom is alive and healthy, I will have a patient life partner who protects and provides, is emotionally available, communicates well, and loves me in the way that I need to be loved. By doing this I have just sent out gratitude for many things to the universe ("Give Thanks" by India.Arie and "Grateful" by Chris-n-Teeb).

Self-Reflection

To ensure you understand the book of meditation and recognize what is at stake if you do not pursue inner peace and the purpose of your life, reflect on the following:

- How can I integrate grounding exercises in my life to remain present every moment?

- How can I establish a habit of meditation to get necessary answers to move forward?

- What can I do to exercise my creative muscle?

- What can I start, stop, and keep doing to maintain proper posture throughout life?

- What must I do to create a habit of making consistent and conscious choices rooted in positive intent that aligns with what I am trying to manifest, hopefully peace and purpose?

Grounding Exercise Practice

Routinely practice these steps with a few of your senses to pull yourself into the present moment.

You need the following:

- Hearing: Water, chimes, or any instrumental sounds that are not distracting

- Smell: A candle, incense, or something that gives off a scent that you enjoy

- Touch: A necklace, bracelet, or object that has a texture that you can identify

Do the following:

- Hearing: Play the sound of choice at a comfortable volume

- Smell: Safely place your scented object within smelling distance

- Touch: Grab your object and get comfortable in a safe space

- Focus heavily on your senses (hearing, smell, and touch) with your eyes closed while practicing slow and deep breathing

After doing this for a few minutes, your mind should be still. Welcome to the present moment.

Transition to Abundance

The consistent and conscious choice of inner peace and chasing purpose leads to everything one could desire during this human experience. One would not grow deeply attached to desired worldly things through inner peace. One would realize that the essential things that withstand time, space, and energy are purpose-based and are more fulfilling than desired worldly things. I am not saying that one shouldn't acquire worldly things but should instead be mindful of intent and attachment, as we know there is always a more profound reason for our behaviors. In this phase of our human experience, when it is a societal norm to acquire worldly things, we must set ourselves and future generations up for success.

We must preserve the freedom of choice to choose a life of peace and purpose for future generations. As mentioned at the beginning of this workbook, choosing a life of peace and purpose yields abundance in many forms, not just materially. Opportunities for relationships, learning, and experiencing life can create a sense of family and deep connection within the greater community, a united voice that cuts through many unnecessary noises created by the systems at work. I intend to use the abundance, in all forms, that is inevitably coming to me for a positive change, freeing people's minds so they can operate at their highest potential through self-awareness. Waves of self-aware people that demonstrate good mental health practices and educate themselves to think independently; my purpose is being fulfilled.

Do the Work

What's at Stake?

Now that you have completed this workbook, reflect on what is at stake if you continue to do what you have done that may not align with peace and purpose. Take at least fifteen minutes to journal about the impacts of your decisions before completing this workbook, what you will do differently, and what is at stake if you do not choose peace and purpose.

Write a Letter to Yourself

Now that you have completed this workbook and recognize what's at stake if you do not choose peace and purpose, write a few letters to yourself.

- Write a letter to the you that helped you get to where you are.

- Write a letter to you with the new perspective on life uncovered from this book and the knowledge of how to help you get to the life you deserve through peace and purpose.

- Write a letter to you stating what you want to be true.

Write a Letter to Future Generations

Now that you recognize what is at stake and have written letters to yourself, write a few letters to future generations.

- Write a letter to future generations about what you wish you knew before you started on this journey of peace and purpose.

- Write a letter to future generations that could use your work from this workbook as a compass for their life, hopefully to obtain peace and purpose.

- Write a letter to future generations about what you want to be true for their lives.

Conclusion

I hope you see why a journey of peace and purpose is necessary to live the life you deserve. Peace is found when you embrace the core of who you are. You recognize that even with your imperfections, you are divine perfection. Without you being your authentic self and acknowledging your imperfections, your purpose could never come forth. Through our lived experiences, we are readied for our purpose, molded and shaped by our circumstances and the people in our lives. We can pour our gift into the world through our gifts, talents, and being of service to people.

As an imperfect vessel that is divine perfection, we can only honor our purpose as long as we have the capacity necessary to do so. Knowing that you can leverage the power of the creator of this human experience to co-create your life is life changing. Hopefully, this workbook has equipped you with a new perspective on life, how to better navigate this human experience from a place of peace, and the desire to chase your purpose in life, given your decisions have impact beyond future generations and what your mind can fathom. It's never been about being perfect but consistent during the journey of peace and purpose. What will you do now?